The Road to Damascus

Kairos and Conversion

First published July 1989
Catholic Institute for International Relations (CIIR),
22 Coleman Fields, London N1 7AF, UK,
Center of Concern, 3700 13th Street,
N.E. Washington, D.C. 20017, USA
and Christian Aid, PO Box 100, London SE1 7RT, UK

Second edition published January 1990
Catholic Institute for International Relations (CIIR) and Christian Aid

ISBN 1 85287 062 1

Cataloguing in Publication Data available from the
British Library

Cover design by Jan Brown Designs
Typeset and printed by Russell Press Ltd

Contents

Introduction

The Road to Damascus was launched in southern Africa, Central America and Asia in the middle of July 1989. In South Africa Archbishop Desmond Tutu and leading churchmen held a press conference, in the Philippines there was a symbolic signing of a thirty-foot scroll and a march to a Manila monument to three priests killed by the Spaniards, and in Nicaragua Father Ernesto Cardenal read from the document at an international Christian gathering celebrating the country's tenth anniversary of liberation from the Somoza dictatorship. In each of these countries the document was published in booklet form with numerous signatories. Those who signed were drawn from a wide variety of churches, Christian organisations and movements, and basic Christian communities.

In late July representatives from the three regions came to London and Washington to proclaim and draw attention to the document. Press conferences were held in the Jerusalem Chamber of Westminster Abbey and in the Washington Press Centre. CIIR, Christian Aid and the Center of Concern produced a first international edition of the document for this purpose which, of necessity, did not contain the names of signatories. The document was given considerable publicity in both secular and religious mass media, with South African television explaining and attacking it in an in-depth news item. Within three months it had been widely distributed around the world with translations in Dutch, German and Portuguese, as well as the original Spanish, English and Korean, available through church agencies.

Since July 1989, thousands more Christians have signed the document, and it has had to be reprinted in both the UK and USA. No changes have been made to the original text. This second international edition contains the original text and also the names of the first signatories — those who had signed before the document was launched.

Preamble

We, the signatories of this document, are Christians from different church traditions in seven different nations: the Philippines, South Korea, Namibia, South Africa, El Salvador, Nicaragua and Guatemala. What we have in common is not only a situation of violent political conflict, but also the phenomenon of Christians on both sides of the conflict. This is accompanied by the development of a Christian theology that sides with the poor and the oppressed and the development of a Christian theology that sides with the oppressor. This is both a scandal and a crisis that challenges the Christian people of our countries.

Although the phenomenon is much the same in each of our countries, the two antagonistic forms of Christianity are referred to with a variety of different names; liberation theology, black theology, feminist theology, minjung theology, theology of struggle, the Church of the poor, the progressive church, basic Christian communities, on the one hand; and the religious right, right-wing Christianity, state theology, the theology of reconciliation, the neo-Christendom movements and anti-communist evangelicals, on the other hand. In each of our nations we shall have to spell out exactly which groups of Christians we are referring to. Whatever difference of terminology there may be, the conflict and division among Christians is basically the same in each of our countries.

The purpose of this document is not simply to deplore the divisions among Christians or to exhort both sides to seek unity. We wish to lay bare the historical and political roots of the conflict (Chapter 1), to affirm the faith of the poor and the oppressed Christians in our countries (Chapter 2), to condemn the sins of those who oppress, exploit, persecute and kill people (Chapter 3), and to call to conversion those who have strayed from the truth of Christian faith and commitment (Chapter 4). The time has come for us to take a stand and to speak out.

The road ahead is like the road to Damascus along which Saul was travelling to persecute the first generation of Christians. It was along this road that he heard the voice of Jesus calling him to conversion. We are all in continuous need of self-criticism and conversion. But now the time has come for a decisive turnabout on the part of those groups and individuals who have consciously or unconsciously compromised their Christian faith for political, economic and selfish reasons.

Hundreds of Christians have been involved in the preparation of this document, and thousands of us have chosen to sign it. Extensive research and consultation within each of our countries and weeks of dialogue between representatives from the seven countries were conducted over a period of two and a half years. The results of all this work are presented here as a proclamation of faith and a call to conversion.

Chapter One

The Roots of Our Conflict

1. As Christians, we look at our situation with eyes that have read the Bible stories. According to the Bible, violent conflict began when Cain killed his brother Abel despite the fact that they had just offered sacrifices together to the same God (*Gen 4: 3-8*). Israel was born as a people of God in struggle against the power of Egypt. It had to confront the great empires of ancient times, the Assyrians, the Babylonians, the Greeks and the Romans. The prophets were often in conflict with the kings of Israel when they saw that the people were treated unjustly. Jesus preached a message that incurred the ire of the religious authorities, who handed him over to the Roman procurator to be crucified.

2. The early Christians were considered a threat by the Roman empire; they were persecuted and martyred. Then in the 4th century, under Emperor Constantine, Christianity became the official religion of the empire. In the hands of the ruling powers it became a weapon for legitimising the expansion of the empire and, later, the colonisation of peoples.

Colonialism

3. Except in the case of Korea which was colonised by Japan, the European nations that colonised our countries pride themselves on being Christian. Conquest and evangelisation, colonisation and the building of churches advanced together. The cross blessed the sword which was responsible for the shedding of our people's blood. The sword imposed the faith and protected the churches, sharing power and wealth with them.

4. As a result of "discovery and conquest", millions of people have been killed; indigenous populations have been eliminated; entire civilisations and cultures have been destroyed. Millions have been enslaved, uprooted from their native land, deculturised and deprived of their wealth and resources. Women and children have been victims of additional and distinct oppression. Natural resources have been

exploited and abused to such an extent that they cannot be replenished.

5. One of the most serious and lasting legacies of European colonialism is racism. In South Africa it has been institutionalised and legalised in the form of the notorious system of apartheid.

People Against Colonialism

6. The history of our people is not only a history of oppression and suffering; it is also a history of struggle. The first stories of resistance come from the indigenous people and communities. The colonisers had superior weapons and the indigenous communities often fought separately instead of together, but they resisted, sometimes to the very last member of the community. Others withdrew deeper into the mountains to preserve what was left unconquered by the invaders.

7. From within the womb of colonialism, those who were initially conquered eventually rose in rebellion, and in some cases overthrew colonial rule through revolution. There were many battles and few lasting victories, but the prophets and martyrs of the people established a tradition of resistance.

8. Although Christianity was part and parcel of colonial rule, Christians were also to be found on the side of the people who fought against colonialism. In Latin America, during the first centuries of colonisation, missionaries and even bishops added their own to the voices of protest, to the extent of denying the Spanish crown the right to expropriate the land of indigenous people and to put them under foreign authorities. In Korea Christians fought for national independence against Japanese colonialism.

Western Imperialism

9. Today, most Third World countries are no longer colonies, but we are still dominated by one or more imperial power — the United States, Japan and Western Europe. Their web of economic control includes an unfair international trade system, multinational companies that monopolise strategic sections of our economy, economic policies dictated by lending banks and governments

together with the International Monetary Fund and the World Bank. Even technology is used as a tool for domination. The staggering size of Third World debt is only one dramatic sign of our subordination to imperialism.

10. In some of our countries imperialism violates national sovereignty by establishing military bases with nuclear weapons that endanger our people's lives. Various methods of political intervention subvert our independence, usually with the cooperation of local rulers. Our educational system, mass media, religious and cultural institutions reproduce a subservient colonial mentality; this is reinforced by Western habits of consumption.

11. Imperialism uses the tactic of divide and rule. It supports governments that discriminate against people and treat them unjustly because of their race or colour. It reinforces sexism and the subordination of women. It sometimes widens the divisions even among the elite but more often it seeks to unite the ruling elite against the people. In most countries this leads to the establishment of what is today called the **national security state**.

12. The effects of imperialism upon the Third World form a litany of woes: our children die of malnutrition and disease, there are no jobs for those who want to work, families break up to pursue employment abroad, peasants and indigenous communities are displaced from their land, most urban dwellers have to live in unsanitary slums, many women have to sell their bodies, too many die without having lived a life that human persons deserve. We also suffer because of the plunder of our natural resources, and then we ourselves are being blamed for it.

People Against Imperialism

13. The tradition of popular resistance lives on in our countries. Even though most of our ruling elite collude with imperialism to deceive and divide the people, groups and communities manage to reflect critically on their oppression and organise themselves. Communities of peasants and indigenous people, workers and slum dwellers — men, women and children — struggle for their own immediate needs and also for shared long-term issues. In much the same way, students, youth and teachers, church people and cultural workers, doctors,

nurses, lawyers and members of other professions, including some business people, become part of the mass democratic movement.

14. As this movement becomes more widespread and organised, the power and wisdom of ordinary people develops and deepens. They recall lessons from history, learn from their mistakes and achievements, and experience solidarity. They exchange insights about the nature of imperialism and its many disguises. Going beyond protest and resistance, they assume responsibility for proposing and pursuing a people's alternative to the present system. They do not have illusions that the struggle will be easy or quick, but also do not shirk sacrifice because they have hope.

15. This movement of organised and conscious people marks the coming of age of a new historical subject. As we exchange our stories not only within our countries but among different countries, we also learn the many names we give to this new creation — the people, *el pueblo*, *minjung*, *ang sambayanan*.

16. As Third World people, we focus on Western imperialism and what is called North-South relations, but we are aware of other important conflicts in the world. There is the East-West conflict between industrial capitalist countries and socialist countries. There are conflicts within capitalist countries and among capitalist countries; the same is true of socialist countries.

17. Western imperialism tries to force our struggle for national liberation into an East-West framework. Let us be clear that we know about the wrongdoings of the East, both within socialist countries themselves and in their relation to other Third World countries. But what we experience directly is domination by the West and we do not want to be drawn into the East-West conflict.

18. Socialist countries are admitting their mistakes and addressing the need for reforms. The United States and the Soviet Union both declare that they want to slow down and even reverse the arms race, and talk of negotiations to solve regional conflicts. All these are welcome pronouncements. Ironically, just when there is talk of more peaceful coexistence between East and West, our countries in the South experience increased hostile attacks from the West.

Low Intensity Conflict and Total War

19. Colonial and imperial powers have reacted to the people's resistance by devising different counter-insurgency programmes. Faced with the emergence of Third World people as new historical subjects, they have developed what they consider a more sophisticated response. It has different names — low intensity conflict (LIC), low intensity war, total war, total strategy, total security.

20. For the imperialists, it might be low intensity conflict, but for the Third World people it is total war. LIC uses all military weapons, short of nuclear arms. It employs not just rifle infantry, but artillery, helicopter gunships, armoured vehicles like casspirs in South Africa and Namibia and armadillos in Central America; it does not hesitate to bomb suspected rebel areas. It organises paramilitary groups, death squads and vigilantes to divide and destroy unarmed communities and organisations of the people.

21. Unlike traditional regular warfare, total war places a premium on psychological and ideological war. In Namibia and South Africa, this is called "winning hearts and minds" or WHAM. The Santa Fe Document calls it "cultural war". It tries to discredit all those who work for change by calling them "communists", while trying to present the government as democratic. In highly repressive and polarised situations, it promotes reformist alternatives, or a "third force". This total strategy includes the misuse of Christianity as a religious legitimation for the West.

Christians in Conflict

22. The misuse of Christianity in the ideological war is imperialism's response to an earlier development — the good news of Christian participation in the suffering and struggle of the people.

23. Some Christians started by immersing themselves in communities of the oppressed and then came to understand their faith as a commitment to solidarity. For other Christians, involvement came as their response to an imperative of faith, the fruit of reflection in basic Christian communities. However different their paths may have been, their participation developed into a more organised and conscious direction. They took up whatever tasks needed to be done

within the people's movement, but they also sought to release the power and resources of their faith and church to serve the poor.

24. This new development has caused grave concern in the highest circles of imperialist leaders. The organised and conscious presence of Christians in the people's movement is not only one more addition to the ranks of those who struggle against the system of domination; it weakens the capacity of imperialism to use Christianity to defend the Empire.

25. No wonder then that formal proposals for a systematic attack on theology of liberation have been presented to the president of the United States, as in the Santa Fe Documents I and II. New institutions have been established to develop a theology that defends imperialism. Joint projects are launched with some Third World governments and security agencies to infiltrate the Church, coopt conservative Christians and "neutralise" progressive ones. Christianity is interpreted to suit these purposes while the theology of liberation is accused of being political.

26. Christian faith has now been introduced into the political conflict. Both oppressor and oppressed seek religious legitimation. Both sides invoke the name of God and of Jesus Christ, and Christians are found on both sides of the political conflict in most of our seven countries.

27. Nor does the matter end there. The political conflict has now entered into the Churches. The Church itself has become a **site of struggle**. Some sectors of the Church align themselves with the status quo and defend it passionately, while others align themselves with the oppressed and struggle for change. There are yet others who claim to be neutral. In fact neutrality plays into the hands of those in power because it enables them to continue and to discredit the Christians who oppose them. Neutrality is an indirect way of supporting the status quo.

28. There is nothing new about religious conflict as such. Christians or believers in the God of the Bible have been on opposing sides in political conflicts before. What is new today is the intensity of the conflict and the awareness we have of it. Never before have we been so conscious of the political implications of Christian faith. This religious conflict is not a mere academic debate, it is a matter of life

and death. What is at stake is the future of justice, peace, freedom, and the glory of God.

29. The conflict among Christians raises some very serious questions which we shall have to address in the rest of this document:
Is the God invoked by both sides the same God?
Is God on both sides?
If not, on whose side is God?
What has been revealed to us about God in Jesus?

Chapter Two

The Faith of the Poor

30. The God whom the missionaries preached was a God who blessed the powerful, the conquerors, the colonisers. This God demanded resignation in the face of oppression and condemned rebelliousness and insubordination. All that was offered to us by this God was an interior and other-worldly liberation. It was a God who dwelt in heaven and in the Temple but not in the world.

31. The Jesus who was preached to us was barely human. He seemed to float above history, above all human problems and conflicts. He was pictured as a high and mighty king or emperor who ruled over us, even during his earthly life, from the heights of his majestic throne. His approach to the poor was therefore thought of as condescending. He condescended to make the poor the objects of his mercy and compassion without sharing their oppression and their struggles. His death had nothing to do with historical conflicts, but was a human sacrifice to placate an angry God. What was preached to us was a completely other-worldly Jesus who had no relevance to this life.

32. These were the images of God and Jesus that we inherited from our conquerors and the missionaries who accompanied them. In some cases these beliefs were imposed upon us at the point of the sword and some of our ancestors were forcibly baptised. In the case of Korea, European missionaries came without colonisation. It was only later that we discovered that this God and this Jesus had been formed in the image and likeness of European kings, emperors and conquerors.

33. Gradually our experience of poverty and oppression began to raise questions for us: Why does God allow us to suffer so much? Why does God always side with the rich and the powerful? Some of us began to see that these questions were also raised in the psalms and in the book of Job who refused to accept any easy answers. Was poverty and oppression really the will of God?

34. In time we began to realise that we could never expect justice from our oppressors. After many years of protest and pleading we began to take responsibility for our own liberation. We began to organise ourselves and became a people, the subjects of our own history, *el pueblo, minjung. Minjung* is the Korean word for the people as opposed to the ruling powers when they become conscious of themselves as subjects who can decide for themselves instead of being mere objects to be ruled and governed.

35. The Christians who were part of this development began to read the Bible with new eyes. We were no longer dependent upon the interpretations of our oppressors.

36. What we discovered was that Jesus was one of us. He was born in poverty. He did not become incarnate as a king or nobleman but as one of the poor and oppressed. He took sides with the poor, supported their cause and blessed them. On the other hand, he condemned the rich. "Blessed are you who are poor" (*Lk 6:20*) "Woe to you who are rich" (*Lk 6:24*). He even described his mission as the liberation of the downtrodden (*Lk 4:18*). That was the very opposite of what we had been taught.

37. At the heart of Jesus' message was the coming of the Reign of God. We discovered that Jesus had promised the Reign of God to the poor: "Yours is the Reign of God" (*Lk 6:20*) and that the good news about the coming of God's Reign was supposed to be good news for the poor (*Lk 4:18*).

38. The Reign of God is not simply a way of speaking about the next world. The Reign of God is this world completely transformed in accordance with God's plan. It is like the Jubilee year of Leviticus 25 when all those who are living in slavery will be set free, when all debts will be cancelled and when the land will be restored to those from whom it was stolen. The Reign of God begins in this life but stretches out beyond this life. It is transcendent and eschatological without being unconcerned about the problems and suffering of the poor in this life.

39. In preaching the Reign of God Jesus was prophesying the coming of a new world order. This brought him into conflict with the status quo of his time, the religious and political authorities. They found his preaching "subversive". That is why they conspired to kill him.

40. Jesus was and still is the Word of God, the true image of God. The poor and the oppressed Christians of today, together with those who have taken an option for the poor, can now see the true face of God in the poor Jesus -persecuted and oppressed like them. God is not an almighty oppressor. The God we see in the face of Jesus is the God who hears the cries of the poor and who leads them across the sea and the desert to the promised land (*Ex 3:17*). The true God is the God of the poor who is angry about injustice in the world, vindicates the poor (*Ps 103:6*), pulls down the mighty from their thrones and lifts up the lowly (*Lk 1:52*). This is the God who will judge all human beings according to what they have done or not done for the hungry, the thirsty, the naked, the sick and those in prison (*Mt 25:31-46*).

41. We are grateful to God for the grace that has enabled us to rediscover God in Jesus Christ. "I bless you Father for hiding these things from the learned and the clever and revealing them to mere children" (*Lk 10:21*). It is by the Spirit of God that we have been able to see what the learned and the clever were not able to see. We no longer believe in the God of the powerful and we want no gods except the God who was in Jesus. "I am Yahweh your God who brought you out of the land of Egypt, out of the house of slavery. You shall have no gods except me" (*Ex 20:1-2*).

42. With this new faith in Jesus, we can now begin to read the signs of our times, discern the presence of the risen Jesus in our midst, appreciate the action of the Holy Spirit and see our present conflict with new eyes. We are no longer surprised to discover that the followers of Jesus are crucified and killed. Now we hear God's voice, especially in the cry of the poor, in the cry of pain and protest, of despair and hope.

43. God is on the side of the poor, the oppressed, the persecuted. When this faith is proclaimed and lived in a situation of political conflict between the rich and the poor, and when the rich and the powerful reject this faith and condemn it as heresy, we can read the signs and discern something more than a crisis. We are faced with a **kairos**, a moment of truth, a time for decision, a time of grace, a God-given opportunity for conversion and hope.

Chapter Three

Our Prophetic Mission

44. Throughout history, we Christians have often been deaf to God's voice and blind to God's presence in people. This lack of faith has prevented us from exercising the prophetic mission that Jesus has given us. We have often been silent instead of denouncing injustice and oppression. Instead of working for justice and liberation, we have often remained uninvolved.

45. How shall we explain this silence and uninvolvement, this blindness and unbelief? For some of us, the reason lies in a life that is not confronted by the suffering and struggle of the poor, and therefore the choice of a convenient God who does not challenge us to take part in a movement for change. For others, however, the reason lies in a choice of privilege and power, and a **conscious** defence of the status quo. In many cases, it includes taking part in attacks against movements for change, in repression and the killing of the poor.

46. For such people, it is not simply an inability to see and hear; it is a refusal to see and hear. It is not merely lack of faith in the God of life; it is the worship of a false god — the sin of idolatry.

47. Although we are conscious of our own sins, we must raise our voice in the denunciation of this sin. It is a sin that serves the total war being waged against the people, leading to the death and destruction of our communities.

48. The sin of idolatry lies at the heart of the imperialism of money. In choosing to serve the idols of death rather than the God of life, Christianity is used as a weapon against the people. Idolatry leads Christians to other sins — heresy and apostasy, hypocrisy and blasphemy.

Idolatry

49. Idolatry is the sin of worshipping or being subservient to someone or something which is not God, treating some created thing as if it were a god. "They worshipped and served the creature instead of the Creator" (*Rm 1:25*). In the Old Testament Moses and the prophets condemned the worship of the golden calf, the Baals and other idols made by human hands (*Ex 20:4-5; Ps 115:4*). In New Testament times the principal form of idolatry was the worship of mammon (*Mt 6:24; Lk 16:13*).

50. The same is true for us today. In our countries, the worship of money, power, privilege and pleasure has certainly replaced the worship of God. This form of idolatry has been organised into a system in which consumerist materialism has been enthroned as a god. Idolatry makes things, especially money and property, more important than people. It is **anti-people**.

51. Because the idol is anti-people, it **demands absolute submission and blind obedience**. The idols we read about in the Bible make their followers into slaves, prisoners or robots depriving them of freedom. Subservience to money dehumanises people. Profits are pursued at the expense of people. The graven image of the god of money today is the national security state that defends the system and demands absolute and blind obedience. In some countries, it is cruel and merciless; in others, it wears a deceptive mask. Those who disobey are punished brutally; those who obey are rewarded with material benefits and security. Idols rule by fear and intimidation or by trying to buy people, to bribe them and seduce them with money.

52. Idolatry is the **denial of all hope for the future**. The idols of the past were worshipped by people who were afraid of change, who wanted things to remain the same, who did not want a future that was different, who found their security in the status quo. The same is true today. Those who benefit from the status quo live in total fear of any real transformation. They are at the service of the status quo and will go to any lengths to make it secure.

53. It was for the sake of **security** that the people of ancient times turned to the Baals and other idols. Today, our oppressors turn to money and military power and to the so-called security forces. But their security is our insecurity. We experience their security as

intimidation and repression, terror, rape and murder. Those who turn to the idols for security demand our insecurity as the price that must be paid. They fear us as a threat to their security.

54. Idolatry demands a **scapegoat**. The idolaters believe that some people or groups of people must be blamed for all that goes wrong in a society so that by driving out or killing the scapegoat, they can feel purged and exonerated of their guilt. This is an idolatrous way of dealing with guilt and achieving atonement. Often enough, perfectly innocent people are sacrificed as scapegoats, though it may sometimes happen that the scapegoat is not entirely innocent, like the woman taken in adultery in John 8:2-11.

55. The worshippers of money in our countries use communism or socialism of any kind or even suspected leanings in that direction as their scapegoat. The guilt that they feel and the sins that they commit are projected onto this convenient scapegoat, that then can be blamed for all that is wrong or might go wrong in the future. Thus violence, disregard for human rights, repression and brutality are talked about as the characteristics of communists. It then becomes perfectly justifiable to harass, imprison, torture and even kill them. They have become scapegoats.

56. In this way it also becomes possible to justify the persecution of the Church. Certain people in the Church, progressive groups or, in some places, Church leaders, are labelled "communists", to separate them from other Christians and turn them into scapegoats who can then be discredited, hated, denounced, silenced and even eliminated.

57. The idols demand **human sacrifices**. This is what angered the prophets most of all about the worship of the Baals. Jeremiah deplored the superstitious belief that the gods can only be placated by the sacrifice of children (*Jer 19:4-5*). Today this is still the most evil dimension of the sin of idolatry in our countries. People, young and old, innocent and defenceless, are being sacrificed to placate mammon — the national security state and international capitalism.

58. We live with the everyday reality of human sacrifice: starving children, deaths in detention, assassinations, massacres and disappearances. The killing of people has become a kind of religious ritual, a necessary part of the total war on people.

59. Idolatry is **fanatical**. It encourages irrational and unrestrained behaviour. We see this in the massacres of people by soldiers, policemen and death squads, *contras* and vigilantes. We see it also in their demented hatred of those who resist and their frenzied persecution of church persons when they protest. It is impossible to be reasonable when you submit to the idols of money, power, privilege and pleasure. The idols create bloodthirsty feelings that the system itself cannot control.

60. Idolatry is a **lie** and it can only continue by deceiving people more and more. The fundamental lie is making material things more important than people. Scapegoating is a lie. Presenting all real change as communist and therefore atheist is a lie.

61. Idolatry's propaganda is a series of lies. It presents the existing order as the natural order of things and radical change as chaos. It coopts the words that people use to describe their aspirations, like peace, democracy and freedom, and makes them mean something different. Peace comes to mean preserving the status quo. Democracy is used to describe the manipulation of national elections, apartheid elections for local government as in South Africa, or a mechanism to ensure that the majority of the people do not have access to real power. Freedom means giving the rich and powerful the opportunity to exploit and manipulate others. Idolatry disguises the truth and creates a whole culture of lies. Satan, as Jesus says, is the father of lies (*Jn 8:44*).

Heresy

62. The word heresy means **choice**. A heresy is a form of belief that selects some parts of the Christian message and rejects other parts, in such a way that those doctrines which are selected for belief become themselves distorted.

63. The theological justification of apartheid in South Africa has been declared a heresy. It is recognised by most Christians today to be a distortion of God's revelation. But we would like to take this famous declaration further: we denounce all forms of right-wing Christianity as heretical.

64. Right-wing Christianity under whatever name is a way of believing that rejects or ignores parts of God's revelation and selects or distorts other parts in order to support the ideology of the national security state. We are convinced that this heretical choice is made for selfish political purposes, although not all the adherents of right-wing Christianity are necessarily aware of this. Consequently right-wing Christianity is the conscious or unconscious legitimation of idolatry.

65. Right-wing Christianity is being promoted with vigorous and expensive campaigns in all our countries and in almost all Christian traditions: Catholic, Reformed, Lutheran, Anglican, Evangelical and Pentecostal.

66. One of the characteristics of this new heresy is that it denies Christian freedom by insisting upon blind obedience to authority. The famous text from Romans 13 is misused to demand unquestioning and uncritical allegiance to the political authorities who exercise the politics of death and deception. Similarly, in some countries Christians are commanded to submit themselves blindly to the absolute authority of church leaders.

67. Right-wing Christianity replaces Christian responsibility and trust in God with submission to the yoke of slavery. It promotes authoritarianism and domination in the family and society. It often distorts even the authority of the Bible by treating it as a book from heaven that must be obeyed without understanding or critical comprehension. In some countries, this is called fundamentalism. The attempt to find security in blind obedience, absolute certainties and submission to authoritarianism is not faith. It is slavery. "For freedom Christ has set us free; stand fast therefore, and do not submit again to the yoke of slavery" (*Gal 5:1*).

68. Another characteristic of right-wing religion is that it takes some of the valid distinctions made by Christianity e.g. between body and soul, material and spiritual, this world and the next, politics and religion, the profane and the sacred, society and the individual and turns them into antagonistic **dualisms**. It creates polarisation and antagonism between the body and the soul, the material and the spiritual. This is against Christian teaching since the Bible reveals only one God creator of the material and the spiritual, the individual and the social. We must not "put asunder what God has put together".

69. It is not without reason that right-wing Christians believe in antagonistic dualisms. It prevents the spiritual from influencing their material lives, it keeps God out of their political and economic interests. They say that they are only interested in the soul, but in fact they are very concerned about the political and economic status quo. They want to preserve it at all costs because it benefits them. They say we must keep religion out of politics but invoke a kind of religion that supports the status quo. They reduce salvation to that of the soul only.

70. This leads to an other-worldly interpretation of the Bible. Everything in the Bible that refers to material possessions, wealth and poverty, oppression and liberation is distorted and made to refer only to other-worldly and individualistic concerns. This spiritualistic interpretation of the Bible is reductionist.

71. A further characteristic of right-wing Christianity is that it is fanatically **anti-communist**. It one-sidedly identifies Christianity with capitalist values of individualism and competition while rejecting the Christian values of equality and cooperation, saying that these are communist and socialist values. Communism, whatever real faults it may have, is then used as a **scapegoat**. The war against communism is treated as a holy war or crusade. Christian values like loving your enemy, forgiving seventy times seven times, compassion, solidarity and calling the sinner to conversion are conveniently forgotten once a person or group is labelled "communist" or "subversive".

Apostasy

72. Apostasy goes much further than heresy. It abandons the Christian faith altogether. In the past, those who apostatised from the Christian faith gave up the name "Christian". But today it would not be strategic for the worshippers of the idol to admit that they are no longer Christians. For convenience they still call themselves Christians and continue formally professing the Christian faith, but in fact they no longer believe, much less live, the gospel of Jesus Christ.

73. That they are not just heretical Christians but apostates becomes unmistakably clear when they begin to **persecute** the Church. They

discredit priests and pastors, nuns and theologians, church leaders and Christian communities, harass them, sometimes imprison them, torture and kill them. When the Church and its theology is seen as a dangerous threat to the national security state and when the Church becomes a target for national security strategy, then it is not just a question of heresy but of apostasy.

74. In some of our countries military chaplains are sent to schools to explain the total war against the people. They arrange camps and conferences for church youth and Sunday school teachers; military men are specially trained to take over catechism classes. Alternative councils of churches are set up, alternative church leaders and churches are promoted to support the national security state.

75. This persecution of Christians also involves vicious attacks upon liberation theology. Right-wing sects are promoted in order to undermine and divide those Churches that take the side of the poor. This is part of an imperialist strategy that does not even bother to keep itself secret; it is spelled out clearly for Latin America in the Santa Fe Documents I and II.

Hypocrisy

76. Jesus issued many strong condemnations of the hypocrisy of the scribes and Pharisees. They did not always practise what they preached. They were not in reality what they appeared to be in public, they were whited sepulchres. Because they were more concerned about their popularity and their reputations than about the truth, they became too cowardly to speak out about the real evils in their society. They strained out gnats while swallowing camels and saw the splinter in someone's eye while overlooking the plank in their own eyes (*Mt 23:24; 7:5*).

77. Is it not true that some Christians and church leaders in our countries are like those scribes and Pharisees? They are very cautious and "prudent" and do not wish to rock the boat. They are either part of the rich and powerful or afraid of them. Even when there are obvious cases of injustice, they do not speak out or do something about it. When hundreds or even thousands "disappear", it is especially hypocritical for church leaders to maintain their

silence. We know that in some cases, this silence is even worse than hypocrisy — it is a mask for their complicity in the "dirty war".

78. There are those who claim to be non-partisan and talk of keeping the balance, but they betray their partisanship by criticising mainly those who question the status quo. They speak of reconciliation and patience, but address this mainly to the victims of the system and the powerless. They promote reforms as a "third way", but restrict people's participation to traditional forms. They profess commitment to democracy, but do not wish the people to exercise power effectively. They warn against the dangers of politicising the Church, but they often compromise the Church through alliances and negotiations with those in power. They accuse progressive Christians of dividing the Church, but in some countries they use their position to force a split between the institutional and the popular Church even denying that some base communities are part of the Church.

79. There is hypocrisy in the use of double standards, while claiming to have only one. For example, there are those who preach absolute non-violence, but while they condemn the armed struggle of the people, they seldom question the use of arms against the people. They recognise the right of self-defence when the state invokes it, but not when the people exercise it. In the case of military forces, they uphold the legitimate use of violence and criticise only its abuse; but when it comes to the people's use of arms, they do not make the same distinction. The ideological reasons for such double standards are exposed by what they say about a state that is socialist, anti-imperialist or progressive. Suddenly, they seem to have no problem at all about the use of violence against such states, even indiscriminate violence. This is a clear case of double standards and hypocrisy.

Blasphemy

80. Idolatry is a sin against the first commandment. Of all the sins related to it, none is more scandalous than the sin against the second commandment — blasphemy. "You shall not utter the name of Yahweh your God to misuse it" (*Ex 20:7*). It is blasphemy to misuse the name of God in defence of imperialism. Theologians of the Institute of Religion and Democracy in the United States of America even compare multinational corporations to the servant of Yahweh.

This sin has deadlier consequences when some bishops and priests become military officers, thereby legitimising the armed forces, and when they publicly bless the weapons of war that are used to kill our people, thereby justifying total war as a holy war. In some countries there are priests who are not only chaplains of the military, they even provide spiritual advice to leaders of death squads. To invoke the name of the God of life to justify death and destruction is blasphemy. It is giving scandal to the little ones (*Mk 9:42; Lk 17:1-2*).

81. In the service of the idols, certain things and persons become sacred. Money and property and, above all, security are sacred. Government and military authorities are like priests of a pseudo-religion. In some countries whites become a sacred people. This too is blasphemy.

82. Blasphemy also takes the form of "satanisation" — attributing the work of the Holy Spirit to the devil. Satanisation refuses to see the God of life in the liberation of the people. It sees the work of liberation as the work of Satan and accuses the people of being possessed by evil spirits. In his time, Jesus was accused of being under the power of Beelzebul precisely when he freed people from evil spirits and healed them. We also remember Jesus' warning about the sin against the Holy Spirit (*Mk 3:22-30*).

Chapter Four

The Call to Conversion

83. The most famous conversion story in the New Testament is the story of the apostle Paul on the road to Damascus. Before his conversion, Saul (as he was then called) persecuted those Jews who had been converted to the way of Jesus. He took sides with the Sanhedrin, the chief priests of the Temple, the scribes and the Pharisees, against Jesus and the people who believed in Jesus. In other words, Saul sided with the authorities and the status quo against this new movement that wanted to "turn the world upside down" (*Acts 17:6*). Saul stood by and approved of the killing of Stephen (*Acts 7:58; 8:1*). Stephen, like Jesus, was seen as a dangerous threat to the Temple and the Law (*Acts 6:14-15*). This was more than a religious conflict because the Temple was the centre not only of religious power but also of political and economic power, while the Law was the guarantee that nothing in that society would change. As far as Saul was concerned, Judaism had to be purged of this new movement in its midst. The disciples of Jesus had to be pursued in every town and village, dragged out and stoned like Stephen.

84. "Saul was still breathing threats to slaughter the Lord's disciples" as he travelled down the road to Damascus armed with letters authorising him to arrest any followers of the Way, men or women, that he could find (*Acts 9:1-2*). Then suddenly it happened. Saul made the startling discovery that he was on the wrong side, that God was on the side of Jesus and that the persecution of the people who followed Jesus was the persecution of Jesus himself.
"Saul, Saul, why do you persecute me?
Who are you, Lord?
I am Jesus whom you are persecuting" (*Acts 9:3-5*).

85. What was revealed to Saul was that God was not on the side of the religious and political authorities who had killed Jesus. On the contrary, God was on the side of the One who had been crucified as a blasphemer, who had been accused of being possessed by Beelzebul, who had been handed over as a traitor, an agitator, a pretender to the throne of David and a critic of the Temple (*Mt 26:*

62,65-66; Lk 23:1-2,5,13). On the road to Damascus Saul was faced with this conflict between these two images or beliefs about God. He was struck blind by it. It was his kairos. Saul became Paul when he accepted in faith that the true God was in Jesus and that the risen Lord was in the very people whom he had been persecuting.

86. This kairos on the road to Damascus must be taken seriously by all who in the name of God support the persecution of Christians who side with the poor. The call to conversion is loud and clear.

87. We must be converted again and again from the idol of mammon to the worship of the true God. We cannot serve two masters, we cannot serve both God and mammon (*Mt 6:24*).

88. Beware of false prophets. They come to us disguised as sheep but inside they are wild wolves. We can recognise what they really are by their fruits (*Mt 7:15-20*). There are false prophets who say there is peace when there is no peace (*Jer 6:14; 8:11; Ez 13:10*). Hear the prophetic voice of those who are being persecuted and oppressed.

89. God is calling us to abandon the practice of making individuals or groups into scapegoats who can be blamed for the very sins that we ourselves commit. Most of all the practice of using communism as a scapegoat must be exposed and rejected. Communist regimes and movements must be criticised too, but they must not be made into scapegoats.

90. We must take seriously Jesus' accusation of hypocrisy. We cannot sit on the fence and profess neutrality while people are being persecuted, exploited and killed. We cannot remain silent because we fear the authorities and do not want to rock the boat. Jesus calls all hypocrites to conversion.

91. All of us who profess to be followers of Jesus of Nazareth are in continuous need of conversion. While we see clearly the idolatry, the heresy, the hypocrisy and the blasphemy of others, we ourselves need to search our own hearts for remnants of the same sins and for signs of triumphalism, self-righteousness, dogmatism, rigidity, intolerance and sectarianism. There should be no place in our hearts for any kind of complacency.

Conclusion

The particular crisis or kairos that has led us to the writing and signing of this proclamation of faith is the conflict between Christians in the world today. We have wished to make it quite clear that those Christians who side with the imperialists, the oppressors and the exploiters of people are siding with the idolaters who worship money, power, privilege and pleasure. To misuse Christianity to defend oppression is heretical. And to persecute Christians who are oppressed or who side with the oppressed is apostasy — the abandonment of the gospel of Jesus Christ.

What we are dealing with here is not simply a matter of morality or ethics. What is at stake is the true meaning of our Christian faith. Who is God? Where is the true Jesus? It is not those Christians who struggle against oppression who are heretics, but those who support the forces of evil and death. The name of God is being blasphemously misused.

This proclamation was written and signed to give an account of the **hope** that is in us. Like the disciples who travelled along the road to Emmaus we are sometimes tempted to give up hope. As the two disciples say: "Our own hope had been that he (Jesus) would be the one to set Israel free" (*Lk 24:21*). What they still had to learn from Jesus and what we need to be reminded of again and again is that the way to freedom and salvation is the way of the cross. "Was it not ordained that the Christ should suffer and so enter into his glory?" (*Lk 24:26*). There is no cheap solution or liberation. There is no easy road.

Because of our faith in Jesus, we are bold enough to hope for something that fulfills and transcends all human expectations, namely, the Reign of God. We are even called to live with the hope that those who collaborate with the idols of death and those who persecute us today will be converted to the God of life.

None of this can happen, however, without pain, suffering and many deaths. Jesus promises us the Reign of God but he also promises that "they will hand you over to the Sanhedrins and scourge you in their synagogues". "You will be dragged before governors and kings." "Brother (and sister) will betray brother (and sister) to death, and the father his child." "You will be hated by all on account of my name" (*Mt 10:17-22*).

The disciple cannot be greater than the master, and we are following the path of a crucified Christ. Whatever twists and turns the road might take, be firm and steadfast. The pain we undergo is part of the birthpangs of a new creation.

The experience of our seven countries working together to compile this document over a period of two and a half years has been an example of solidarity. We hope that such examples of cooperation and dialogue will continue, will develop and will be extended for the benefit of all.

Our oppressors organise themselves nationally and internationally. We cannot afford to face the struggle separately. Solidarity is not optional if we are to promote the cause of God in the world. We call on fellow Christians in the Third World, in industrial capitalist countries and in socialist countries to build a network of exchange and cooperation.

July 1989

Signatures

EL SALVADOR

Associations and groups:

Asociación Bautista de El Salvador
Asociación de jovenes bautistas de El Salvador
Comité del año internacional de solidaridad con Centroamérica Monsenor Romero
Comunidades Cristianas de jóvenes y estudiantes
Comunidad Eclesial de base Rafael Palacios (Santa Tecla)
Comunidades de vida cristiana CVX — El Salvador
Juventud Cristiana por la paz
Iglesia Luterana

Base communities belonging to the movement CEBES (Comunidades Eclesiales de Base de El Salvador):

Ahuachapán (3 communities)
Ayutuxtepeque (5 communities)
La Libertad (Zaragoza)
Morazán (34 communities)
San Antonio Abad (7 communities)
San José Calle Real
San Luis Mariona (5 communities)
San Miguel (6 communities) San Ramón (9 communities)
Santa Ana (2 communities)
Zacamil (15 communities)

Christian communities by department/province:

Chalatenango
Arcatao
Carasque
Las Flores
Guarjila
Honduritas
Nombre de Jesús
Potonico
Quipuré
Quipurito
San Antonio Los Ranchos
Las Vueltas

Cuscatlan
El Barillo
La Bermuda
Copapayo

Estanzuelas
Condadillo
Sitio San Antonio
Tecomatal

Jiquilisco
Aranañas
Marío
Mata de Piña
El Potrero

Salinas
Samorán
Siciguallo

La Libertad
Asuchillo
Las Brumas
Jayaque
Loma Linda
Lourdes
Teotepeque
El Zaite

Nueva Granada Gualcho

Occidente
Capapayo (Armenia)
Cara Sucia
El Congo
La Florida (Texistepeque)
Planes de La Laguna
Potrerillos
Santiago de la Frontera

La Paz
Cuyultitán
Olocuilta

San Salvador
22 Abril
Apopa
Guazapa
El Limón
Madre de los Pobres
Peñalitos
San Roque
Santa Ursula

Sesori
Achotal
Limones
Managuara
Plan del Carao

Usultan
La Barca
Berlín
Hiscatal
Horcones
Mercedes Umaña
Muñoz
Las Puertas
San Francisco
San Simón
Santa Cruz
Tablón
Talpetates
Virginia
Zapotillo

GUATEMALA

José Angel Beltrán, Communidad La Familia
María del Carmen Cruz, Communidad Nueva Alianza
Ricardo Chajal B, Communidad La Familia
Benedicto Coc Chen
Mario René Coy
Luis Divino cicm
Rosita Esquequé, Encuentros Cristianos
P. Marcelino García msc
Gilberto F Godínez, Communidad Corazón de María
P. Lucas Mees cicm
Mario Morales, Encuentros Cristianos
Edgar Pacay Bac
German Paz, Communidad Nueva Alianza
Rigo S Pos, Encuentros Cristianos
José V Ruiz, Encuentros Cristianos
Denis A Smith

Julia Suruy, Communidad Nueva Alianza

Associations:

Asamblea Permanente de Grupos Cristianos: Juanita Camposeco (Directivo), Rosana Elizabeth Rodriguez Elias (Coordinadora), P. José Guerrero (Directivo), Pastor Vitalino Similox (Directivo), Denis Smith (Subcoordinador)

Centro de Estudios, Publicaciones y Servicios de Evangelización (CEPSE)

Centro Evangélico Latinoamericano de Estudios Pastorales (CELEP)

Comunidad de San Martín Cobán, Hermanas ICM

Encuentros Cristianos: Ricardo García (Presidente), Jacobo Lucas (Vice-Presidente), José Guerrero (Secretario General), Nora Coloma (Tesorera), Vocales — Vitalino Similox, Goyita Pirir, Juanita Camposeco.

Fundación Ecuménica Guatemalteca 'Esperanza y Fraternidad' (esfra)

Grupo Monseñor Romero: Juan Carlos Hernández for Grupo Monseñor Romero

Grupo Reconciliación (Ecclesial base communities)

Presbiterio Kakchiquel: José Antonio Otzoy (Pastor Kakchiquel), Vitalino Similox Salazar (Presidente del Presbiterio)

KOREA

Rev. Hong, Keun Soo, Presbyterian Church in the Republic of Korea

Rev. Hong, Seung Hyun, Presbyterian Church of Korea

Rev. Jin, Yon Sub, Mission-Education Centre of Presbyterian Church in the Republic of Korea

Rev. Jun, Byung Ho, Korean Evangelical Church

Rev. Jung, Myung Ki, Korean Methodist Church

Rev. Kang, Won Don, Han-Kuk Theological Study Institute

Rev. Keum, Young Giun, Presbyterian Church of Korea

Rev. Ko, Hyun Young, Presbyterian Church of Korea

Prof. Kim, Chang Nack, Han-Kuk Theological Seminary

Prof. Kim, Kyoung Jae, Han-Kuk Theological Seminary

Mrs. Kim, Kyung Hee, General Secretary of the Women's Association of the Presbyterian Church in the Republic of Korea

Rev. Kim, Yong Bock, Presbyterian Church of Korea

Prof. Noh, Jung Sun, Yonsei University

Rev. Park, Jae Soon, Christian Institute for the Study of Justice and Development

Prof. Park, Jong Wha, Han-Kuk Theological Seminary

Rev. Park, Jong Yul, Presbyterian Church in the Republic of Korea

Mr. Park, Sung Joon, Han-Kuk Theological Study Institute

Rev. Shin, Dae Kyun, Presbyterian Church in the Republic of Korea

Rev. Sohn, Kyoo Tae, Presbyterian Church in the Republic of Korea

Prof. David Suh, Kwang Sun, Ehwa Women's University

Rev. Suh, Kyung Suk, Presbyterian

Church of Korea
Prof. Yoon, Kyung No, Hansung University

NAMIBIA

A. Agapitus, Catholic
M. Agapitus, Catholic
H. Amutenya, Catholic
W. Amuthenya, Catholic
R. Aspara, Catholic
H. Ausiku, Lutheran
J.M. Benz, Lutheran
A. Beukes, Catholic
J.A. Beukes, Apostolic Faith Mission
C.G. Bohitile, Catholic
D.P. Botha, NG Kerk
D.A. Botman, NG Kerk
C. Cloete, Lutheran
P. Cotzee, Catholic
P. Diergaardt, Lutheran
C. Draghoender, Catholic
P. Dunaiski, Apostolic Faith Mission
N. Elago, Lutheran
T. Gideon, Lutheran
O. Hailombe, Anglican
R. Harlech-Jones, Methodist
L. Hausiku, Methodist
A. Iita, Lutheran
R.H. Jones, Methodist
F. Joseph, Apostolic Faith Mission
C. Julius, NG Sendingkerk
J. Kangayi, Lutheran
S. Kavara, Lutheran
Z. Kameeta, Lutheran
M. Kapp, Catholic
K.B. Kathindi, Lutheran
N.E. Kathindi, Anglican
F. Lawrence, Apostolic Faith Mission
A. Lihongo, Lutheran
S.K. Mbambo, Evangelical Reformed Church
A. Mbudje, Catholic
M. Mbudje, Catholic
E. Michael, Catholic
P.D. Munch, Anglican
M.T. Mundjele, Anglican
E. Mwaetako, Anglican
R. Namises, Catholic
B. Namwandi, Anglican
S. Ndeikwila, Lutheran
G. Platt, NG Sendingkerk
H.G. Phatt, NG Sendingkerk
I. Poroto, Catholic
F. Shivute, Lutheran
O. Shivute, Lutheran
J. Sindano, Lutheran
N. Sirongo, Lutheran
L.A. Smith, Lutheran
S. Solomon, Catholic
J.F. Steytler, NG Sendingkerk
P.A. Strydom, Congregational
S.J. Titus, Congregational
P. Tjijombo, Apostolic Faith Mission
D. Tjongarero, Lutheran
G. Totemeyer, Lutheran
H. Tshilongo-Pauly, Lutheran
J.N. van Wyk, Lutheran
H. Wirth, Catholic
T.M. Yates, Anglican

NICARAGUA

Napoleon Alvarado sj, Catholic Church
Rafael Aragón op, Catholic Church
Luz Beatriz Arellano sssf, Catholic Church
Norman Bent, Moravian Church
Enrique Blandón, Waslala, Catholic Church
Gary Campbell, Presbyterian Church
Ernesto Cardenal, Catholic Church

Miguel Angel Casco, Assemblies of God
Antonio Castro, Catholic Church
Edson Castro sdv, Catholic Church
Benjamín Cortes, Church of Christ
Ana María de la Rosa Carpio, Río Blanco Catholic Church
Daniel Driscoll mm, Esquipulas, Catholic Church
Carlos Escorcia junior, Assemblies of God
Xabier Gorostiaga sj, Catholic Church
Socorro Guerrero, Catholic Church
María del Socorro Gutiérrez, Catholic Church
Juan Hernández Pico sj, Catholic Church
Howard Heiner, Methodist Church
César Jerez sj, Catholic Church
Jose Ademar Kaefer sdv, Catholic Church
María López Vigil, Catholic Church
Ana McSweeney mm, Catholic Church
Kenneth Mahler, Bishop, Lutheran Church
Nicanor Mariena, Nazarene Church
Edwin Maradiaga, Catholic Church
Pedro Marchetti sj, Catholic Church
Marllyn Mendez, Baptist Church
Vidaluz Meneses, Catholic Church
Uriel Molina ofm, Catholic Church
Juan Moynihan mm, Jalapa, Catholic Church
Adonis Nino, Christian Mission Church
Edgar Parrales, Catholic Church
Jorge V. Pixley, Baptist Church
Sandra Price snd, Siuna, Catholic Church
Enrique Ramírez, Catholic Church
Carlos Ruiz, Baptist Church
Jerjes Ruiz, Baptist Church
Lisa Schmitt-Culp mm, Ocotal, Catholic Church
Juan Spain mm, Matagalpa, Catholic Church
Carlos Támez, Presbyterian Church
Tomás Téllez, Baptist Church
José María Vigil cmf, Catholic Church
Róger Zavala, Baptist Church
Arnaldo Zenteno sj, Catholic Church
Ricardo Zuñiga, Catholic Church

Associations:

Acción Permanente por la Paz (Witness for Peace) de Nicaragua
Base ecclesial community, San Rafael, Venezuela, Managua
Base ecclesial community, 14 de setiembre, Managua
Base ecclesial community, San Judas, Managua
Base ecclesial community, Primero de Mayo, Managua
Base ecclesial community, Centroamérica, Managua
Base ecclesial communities of El Salvador in Nicaragua (CEBES)
Base ecclesial community, Adolfo Reyes, Managua
Base ecclesial community, Ducualí, Managua
Base ecclesial community, Ciudad Sandino
Base ecclesial community, Enrique Lorente, Managua
Base Christian Community, Nicarao de Managua
Base Christian Community, Riguero de Managua
Base ecclesial community, los Brasiles, Managua
Base ecclesial community, 14 de julio, Managua

Bloque Intercomunitario, Pro-Bienestar Cristiano
CAV — Centro Ecuménico Antonio Valdivieso
CELADEC — Comisión Evangélica Latinoamericana de Educación Centroamérica
CEPA — Centro de Educación y Promoción Agraria
CEPRES — Comisión Evangélica de Promoción de la Responsabilidad Social
Christian communities of El Salvador (CONIP) in Nicaragua
Christian community San Pedro, Estelí (CEBES)
Christian community Monte Tabor (CEBES)
Christian community Estelí (CEBES)
Christian community El Crucero (CEBES)
CIEETS — Centro Intereclesial de Estudios Teológicos y Sociales
CNPPDH — Comisión Nacional de Promoción y Protección de los Derechos Humanos
CODEHUCA — Comisión para la Defensa de los Derechos Humanos en Centroamérica
Comisión de Justicia y Paz OSF de Nicaragua y Centroamérica
Comisión Dominicana de Justicia y Paz de Nicaragua
Comité Ecuménico de Personal Religioso Estadounidense en Nicaragua
Comunidad de Domínicos de Managua
Cooperative Christian community Iván López (CEBES)
Cooperative Christian community San Rafael del Sur (CEBES)
Cooperative Christian community Salina Grande (CEBES)
Cooperative Christian community Omar Torrijos (CEBES)
Coordinación de Comunidades Cristianas de Base de Managua
Coordinated base ecclesial communities of Managua
Grupo de Educación y Comunicación Popular CANTERA
Hermanas Franciscanas OSF de Nicaragua
Iglesia Bautista Genezaret de Managua
Iglesia Evangélica Pentecostal Siloé de Managua
Iglesia Misión Cristiana
Iglesia Luterana Salvadorena en Nicaragua
Iglesia del Nazareno de Managua
IHCA — Instituto Histórico Centroamericano
Instituto de Hermanas Altagracianas en Nicaragua
Movimiento Ecuménico por la Paz, la Vida y la Reconciliación
Parochial Christian community, La Merced de Managua
Seminario Teológico Bautista
TEIOCOIANI — Acción para la Reflexión Teológica y la Formación
UCA — Universidad Centroaméricana de Nicaragua

PHILIPPINES

Bp. Estanislao Q. Abainza, UCCP
Bp. Richard Abellon, PEC
Bp. Ireneo Amantillo, Cssr
Bp. Pat Apura ,UCCP
Bp. Erme Camba, UCCP
Bp. Victor R. Factor
Bp. Antonio Y. Fortich, D.D.

Bp. Gabriel A. Garol, UCCP
Bp. Lorenzo Genotiva, UCCP
Bp. Dinualdo Gutierrez, D.D.
Bp. Julio Xavier Labayen, OCD
Bp. Rafael Lim
Bp. Robert Lee Longid
Bp. Juan Marigsa, UCCP
Bp. T. A. Millamena, PIC
Bp. Wenceslao E. Molato, PIC
Bp. Antonio F. Nepomuceno, OMI
Bp. Tito E. Pasco, PIC
Bp. J. De Dios Pueblos, OMI
Bp. Miguel G. Purungganan
Bp. Alberto B. Ramento, PIC
Bp. Roman B. Tiples Jr., PIC
Bp. Jesus Y. Varela
Bp. (elect) Artemio M. Zabala, PEC
Natividad L. Abao
Fr. Rudy Abao, MSC
Noel B. Abayabay
Fr. Carlos Abesamis, SJ
Rev. Renato Abibico
Rev. Corazon C. Abugan
Cynta Adolfo
Alfie Africa
Sr. Isabel Aggasid
Sr. Annabelle Agila
Pastor Mar A. Aguila
Fr. Hernani A. Aguirre, PIC
Sr. Adela Alcantara
Castor Alejo
Fr Benjamin Alforque, MSC
Isidro C. Alimbuyong, Jr.
Ruben Alinio
Ma. Teresa L. Allones
Rev. Gil N. Almarez
Sr. Teresita Alo
Noli C. Alparce
Sr. Elvira R. Alpas
Imelda F. Alvarez
Rev. Maximo Jr. Alvarez
Dulcena Amar
Francisco Amor, Jr.
Anecito C. Ampis
Josefa Andrada
Pastor Dan P. San Andres
Rev. Elizabeth San Andres, UCCP
Fr. Francis M. Anduyan, PIC
Fr. Harry I. Ang
Sofia Rivera Animo
Bro. Jun Antipuesto
Lucresio L. Anud, Jr.
Rev. Solomon C. Apla-on
Carmelita Apostol
Sr. Vicenta B. Arances
Helen D. Arandia
Manuel D. Arandia
Myrna D. Arandia
Jualito B. Arano
Sr. Carmelita Arenas, RGS
Luis Arueza
Jeanne Asesor
Emmett Asuncion
Rev. David G. Asurto
Emma Valentin Atencio
Sr. Aure, RGS
Billy S. Austin
Sr. Pat Babiera
Sr. M. Kristia Bacani
Pastor Elizabeth Baclao
Mr. Rizaldo I. Bahia
Rev. Rufino Balacang
Sr. M. Roseve Balagat, OSB
Rev. Cordova Balandan, UCCP
Sr.Rosario Balazo, FMM
Sr. Carmen Balazo, FMM
Rev. Fr. Warlito P. Baldomero, PIC
Pastor Eunice P. Pangalayan Baltar
Pastor Arlynne B. Balucio
Glofie G. Baluntong
Ms. Ester Banawis
Sr. Marietta B. Banayo, MA
Sr. Eufrocinia Bandigan,MA
Ms. Nida H. Barcena

Ms. Evelyn H. Barcenas
Ms. Lope R. Bardadillo
Sr. Gavina Barrera, OSA
Mr. Alfredo P. Barro
Ms. Aurora B. Bas
Rev. Emmanuel Bascug, UMC
Eisa Batalla
Mr. Enrique P. Batangan
Sr. Mary Rosario Battung, RGS
Mr. Liberato Bautista, UMC
Sr. Mary Florence Bautista, RGS
Rev. Lito A. Bayao, PEC
Sr. Ma. Cecilia Bayona
Fr. Albert Becher, OMI
Fr. Jovito L. Beguna, MSC
Sr. Mary Ellen Belardo, RGS
Sr. Anita Bello, ICM
Pons Bennagen
Ms. Ma Lourdes M. Berin
Mr. Ramon Ma. Bernabe
Rev. Jose Bailey Bernaldez
Jesus B. Bernales
Fr. Bienvenido Betaizar
Rev. Fr. Ely Bianchi
Fr. Raul M. Biasbas, OMI
Ms. Norma Bidania
Ms. Mildred Krystill R. Bitoy
Jose Bodollo
Sr. Susan Bolanio, UMC
Mario Bolasco
Angelita Bolinas
Rev. Elmer Bolocon, UCCP
Sergio G. Bompat
Rev. Raquel A. Bonachita, UCCP
Fr. Joseph Borreros
Gary Borromeo
Sr. Barbara Bowe, RSCJ
Rev. Nelinda P. Briones
Rev. Sammy P. Briones
Mr. Peter Brock, U.C. (Aus)
Fr. Evelio Buenaflor, Jr.,DCK
Carlos Caalim
Rev. Daniel P. Cabardo Jr., UCCP
Justino Cabazares, Jr.
Fr. Jimmay Cabuntucan
Mr. Alberto Cacayan
Luis Cacayan
Sr. Antonina Cagang, MSM
Fr. Ariston C. Cailing
Ms. Betty Cainap
Sr. M. Celine Cajanding
Fr. Felixberto L. Calang
Ms. Magdalena Calang
Rev. Marilou Calawigan, UCCP
Ms. Lourdes Calleja, O Carm
Josephine Z. Callejo
Eve A. Calunsag
Ms. Nancy Caluya, UMC
Fr. Melner Calvo, DCK
Rev. Ebenezer Camino Sr.
Rev. Alfonso Camiwet, PEC
Ms. Julieta Canja
Rev. Oliver L. Cannen
Fr. Cyril Canning, OMI
Ms. Emma A. Cantor, UMC
Eon A. Capiz
Bro. Dave D. Capucao
Mr. Emilo C. Capulong Jr., UCCP
Rev. Victorino Carillo
Dr. Feliciano Carino, UCCP
Mr. Butch Carpintero
Sr. Carmela Carpio, MM
Rev. Bernardo A. Casiano, UCCP
Ms. Gloria F. Casiano, UCCP
Rev. Wilfredo Casiple, UCCP
Sr. Leontina Castillo, OSA
Ms. Aurora Catalan
Mr. Vicente Catalan
Sr. Alma Christina Catambay,MM
Sr. Ma. Carmeli Catan, OSA
Mr. Mercy B. Cepe
Sr. Ma. Victoria Changcoco, OP
Elizer B. Chavez
Harold R. Chiefe

Sr. Elizabeth Cipriano, CFIC
Ms. Cecilia Ciudadano
Sr. Esperanza Clapano, MA
Mr. Constante D. Claro
Mr. Darlo Claro
Sr. Pablita Claro, O Carm
Ms. Susan Claro
Sr. Irma I. Clavero, MSM
Sr. Mary Clemencia, RGS
Fr. Nestor O. Climaco
Sr. Clarita Clordearta, MA
Fr. Juan B. Colago, DCK
Fr. Frank Connon, CssR
Sr. Patricia A. Conroy,
Fr. Anthony P. Conway, CSsR
Fr. Narciso Coralde
Fr. Reynold G. Corcino
Mr. Yulo Corcino
Rev. Ferdinand Corro, UCCP
Fr. Ramon Cortez
Sr. Natividad F. Cristobal,SCMM
Sr. Corazon Dela Cruz
Sr. Mary Carmela Cruz, RGS
Kent Reynold D. Cue
Sr. Emma Cupin, MSM
Fr. Phil Custodio. MSC
Domingo S. Dalluay, Jr.
Arleen C. Damaso
Sr. Genevieve Damaso,OND
Rev. Edilberto A. Dames
Fr. Ton Danenberg, O' Carm
Ms. Fe Daquida
Mercedita A. Daquis
Sr. Leticia S. Daral, MSM
Rev. Marshall Daul, UCCP
Sr. Christina David, OP
Sr. Julieta A. David, MA
Sr. Mary Amelia David, RGS
Sr. Regina David. ICM
Dorothy Day
Ms. Gloria Dayao
Rev. Eliaquim de Aquino Sr.
Ms. Romea G. de Castro
Mr. Leodegario P. de Castro
Ms. Aileen de Guia
Sr. Bernardita de Jesus, OSA
Bro. Antonio D. de la Cruz, O Carm
Fr. Marciano P. de la Cruz, MSC
Mr. Mario C. de la Cruz
Rev. Pablo de la Cruz, UCCP
Ms. Zenaida B. de la Cruz, UCCP
Edicio de la Torre
Alma A. de Leon
Ms. Rosario I. de Leon
Mr Ephraim de los Santos Sr.
Ms. Nimfa Decena
Sr. Christine Demafelis, MSM
Jeff Demyttenaere
Fr. Lemuel J. Denaga, PIC
Ms. Eleonor Derige
Fr. Rolando E. Detera, MSP
Ms. Merlyn Devillena
Fr. Angelo Diana
Joselito Didal
Anita G. Dimamay
Rev. Luna L. Dingayen
Mr. Maquiling Diosdado
Rev. Norma P. Dollaga, UMC
Elizabeth Dollaga-Julaton
Ms. Olivia Doloja
Gabriel Dolotina
Marivic N. Sto. Domingo
Ms. Elizabeth Dominguez
Rev. Benito Dominguez, UCCP
Mr. Solomon Don
Danilo Doncillo
Rev. Fr. Rojan D. Doronila, MBL
Fr. Roger Duhaylingsod
Fr. Alfonso d. Dujali
Ms. Fe Duldulao, UMC
Sr. Celine Dumas, OND
Sr. Mary John Dumaug, RGS
Fr. Jesus Dumawal,MSC
Ms. SRJ Ruiz Duremdes

Sr. Lydia Ebora, RGS
Mr. Roberto Ecle
Ms. Arsenia C. Elio
Fr. Antonio Elipan
Sr. Eliza, OSB
Fr. Noel C.T. Ello
Ms. Emily B. Elnar
Fr. Romeo Empestan
Rev. Bert Encarnacion
Jaime H. Enriquez
Jo Anne S. Enriquez, UMC
Aris Escobal
Virgilio B. Esguerra
Sr. M. Edita Eslopor
Sr. Gladys Espinosa, ACT
Cynthia C. Espiritu, UMC
Sr. Theresina Estalilla.CFIC
Fr. Jojo Esteban, MSC
Ms. Ada D. Estepa
Mr. Roger B. Estepa, UCCP
Sr. Concepcion Estiandan,MSM
Mr. Dennis Estopace
Sonia Estrella
Fr. Phil Estrella, OMI
Sr. Virginia Fabella
Mr. Samuel A. Fabila
Rev. Fritz Fajardo, UMC
Ms. Luz Fanlo
Rev. Eliseo Fantillaga, UCCP
Fr. Angelito Fausto
Ms. Adela Fazon
Mr. Edgar T. Fernandez
Ms. Cecilia Soon Fernandez
Sr. Cleofe Fernandez, MA
Fr. Jureck Fernandez
Ms. Nena Fernandez
Ms. Jean Marie Ferraris
Ms. Geraldine L. Fiagoy
Ding Flores
Sr. Cecila Fonacier
Ms. Prima Formilleza, CPBC
Rev. Sammie P. Formilleza, CPBC
Eduardo (Eddie) Francisco
Eric Nino Franco
Rev. Ernesto M. Frias, UCCP
Fr. Ramon Fruto, CssR
Jeanette G. Fuellos
Ranela F. de la Fuente
Rev. Caleb Ernane Fuentes, UCCP
Fr. Lolito F. Fuentes
Sr. Rosa Fulleros
Roger Furrer
Fr. Restituto Galang
Fr. Anastacio Galicia
Mr. Alfred Galino, UCCP
Julieta G. Gallos
Nora Galvadores
Constancia L. Gandionco
Rev. Teopisto M. Gange
Sr. Diana Gangoso
Sr. Eustella Garcia
Sr. Frances Pilar Garcia
Nilo Garcia
Rev. Purita O. Garcia
Sr. Remedios Garcia
Pastor Rodolfo A. Garcia
Sr. Zenaida Garcia
Rev. Limerio Garibay, UMC
Sr. Concepcion P. Gasang, MA
Bro. Karl Gaspar, CssR
Danny Gayas
Mario V. Gayta
Sr. Ma. Gloria Geaga, ICM
Sr. Dolores Geier, Maryknoll
John Gelio-Ano
Fr. Henry Gemone, OMI
Sr. Mary Genough, MM
Fr. Peter Geremia, PIME
Mr. Nestor Gerente, UMC
Mr. Ed Gerlock, O Carm
Fr. Efren A. Germintil
Rev. Edwin Gloriane
Sr. Tonnette Go, RGS

Ms. Estella Maris Gonzales
Ms. Madonna Gonzales
Sr. Yolanda Gonzales, FMM
Sr. Mary Vitalis Gorospe, RGS
Fr. Jimwel B. Goyo. MSC
Sr. Helen Graham, Maryknoll
Sr. Angeles Guanco, OSA
Cristin Guanzon
Sr. Lilia Gudmalin, MA
Angel Guerrero
Rev. Ephraim V. Guerrero, UCCP
Felipe I. Guerrero
Merchelbaeh Guido
Sr. Florence Guiwo, CFIC
Sr. Editha D Gujilde, MSM
Sr. Mary Bernadette Guzman, RGS
Fr. Andres Gysberts, MSC
Fr. Primo Hagad, OMI
Sr. Raphael Hernandez
Rev. Larry J. Herrera, UCCP
Fr. Donal Hogan, SSC
Fr. Anton Hoogland, O Carm
Fr. Carmelo Horlador, MSP
Fr. Filivan Hothoved
Rev. Fr. Robert D. Ilay, PIC
Fr. Guillermo L. Ilijay
Rev. Emmanuel Infante, UNIDA
Mr. Perecto Inhog
Fr. Francisco J, Hernando
Mr. Florencio U. Jacela
Ms. Ruth C. Janoras
Sr. Elena Javier, ICM
Fr. Wifredo Jesena, CssR
Ms. Jean B. Joaquin
Mr Senen C. Joaquin Sr.
Sr. Aleli Jose, OP
Fr. Guillermo Juan, Jr., PIC
Rev. Ervin Juit, UCCP
Fr. Rudy N. Juliada
Fr. Romeo Jumao-as, AS
Sr. Lynn Kaum, SCMM
Mr. Frans Kleine Koerkamp
Rev. James Kollin, Jr.
Fr. Peter Kramer, O Carm
Fr. Federico P. Labaglay, OMI
Sr. Evangelina M. Labanda, CFIC
Mr. Eugene Labaro
Fr. Antonio Labiao, Jr.
Sr. Willibrorda G. Laccay, CFIC
Sr. Benigilda Ladia
Denis T. Laguardia
Mr. Floyd P. Lalwet, PEC
Rev. John K. Langbao, PEC
Rev. Fr. Arturo P. Langit
Sr. Pia Lansang, OSB
Mr. John Lansink
Sr. Tessie Lara, ICM
Sr. Lydia L. Lascano, ICM
Ms. Leve S. Laurente
Ms. Melchorita B. Laurente
Fr. Ben Leandicho, OMI
Mr. Montenegro Lemuel
Rev. Reynaldo F. Letana
Ms. Rosa E. Letana
Sr. Leting, MSM
Fr. John Leydon
Ms. Arche Ligo
Sr. Rosalinda Lim, O Carm
Fr. Arnold Lima, Jr.
Mr. Rogelio Lindo
Ms. Anna Theresa Lim Lipata
Ms Rubylin G. Litao
Fr. Gorgonio M. Llubit
Sr. M. Teresa Lopez, SP
Samuel Lorico
Rebecca Lozada
Bro. Willy Lubrico
Rev. Dizon Lucena, UMC
Rev. Harvey M. Lucena, UMC
Sr. Cres L. Lucero, CFIC
Rev. Noel Luces, UCCP
Mr. Ronny Luces, UCCP
Arturo B. Lumagod
Fr. Ven Lumubu-an

Emma Lutao
Ms. Ruth Elynia S. Mabanglo
Boyet Mabunga
Fr. Marcito Macainan, MSC
Begilan Magalina
Sr. Yolanda F. Magana, MSM
Bro. Rogelio Magatol, O Carm
Ms. Liza Gay C. Maglinao
Joel B. Maglunsod
Ms. Emma Magpantay
Prof. Rosalinda Magpantay
Sr. Helen S. Makiling, MSM
Estong Malandac
Fr. Linfred Malapitan, PIC
Sr. Ma. Luz Mallo, MA
Sr. Jean Maloney, Maryknoll
Fr. Robert B. Manansala, OFM
Sr. Mary John Mananzan, OSB
Sr. Fe Mandreza, SCMM
Fr. Jun Mangulabnan, SJ
Mr. Mario R. Mapanao, UCCP
Sr. Remedios Mapinugos, MA
Rev. William B. Mariano
Zaldy Marlaloa
Fr. Thomas Marti, MM
Fr. Michael Martin, SSC
Sr. Asuncion Martinez, ICM
Rev. Rolando C. Martinez, UMC
Mr. Percival Matunog
Mr. Eriberto P. Maureal
Ms. Jasmine B. Maureal
Fr. Piers Maurice, OMI
Benita A. Mayuga
Juanita Mayuga
Fr. Sean McNulty, SSC
Fr. John Meaney, SSC
Sr. Mechtilde
Fr. Paul Medina, O Carm
Mariquita S. Mendoza
Sr. Rosiana Mendoza, ICM
Sr. Victoria Mendoza
Mr. Cornelio Mendriks, O Carm
Fr. Eliseo R. Mercado, OMI
Ranndieh Mercado
Fr. Socrates C. Mesiona, MSP
Agatha Miclat
Gay Miclat
Mr. Arsenia Miguel
Mr. Exo S. Miguel
Sr. Ma. Luz Mijares, OSA
Sr. Toni Milanes, ICM
Danilo Misason
Sr. Carmela Mitaran, OSB
Fr. Mercurio Montenegro, MSC
Ma. Giselle Montero
Sr. Imelda Mora, OSA
Rev. Leonardo Morada
Fr. Ben Moraleda,CssR
Mr. Eden O. Morales, UMC
Mr. Meishach Ruf Morallas
Ms. Wilhelmina A. Morallas
Mr. Ervin More
Rev. Rhodita M. Mostoles, UMC
Orencio Muimar, O. Carm
Rev. Silvino H. Mumar, UCCP
Mr. Adorada Patria Mundo
Patricia M. Munoz
Ms. Aida Jean Nacpil-Manipon, UMC
Mr. Ruben Nalicat
Fr. Feliciano E. Nalzaro Jr., TGB
Fr. Eliseo Napiere, MSP
Ms. Marcelina Naranjo
Victoria Narciso-Apuan
Mr. Zone Narito
Mr. Rey M. Natividad, UCCP
Rev. Gerardo O. Natuel
Atty. Dan J. Navarette
Adele N. Nayal
Ms. Marilyn Negapatan
Ms. Erma P. Ngan
Rev. Ireneo C. Ngoho, UCCP
Roberto D. Nicolasora
Pedro Nieva
Fr. Romeo Nimez, CICM

Rev. Ben A. Nombrado, UCCP
Fr. Thomas O'Brien, MM
Rev. Brendan O'Connell, SSC
Fr. Patrick O'Herlihy, SSC
Fr. Rogelio R. Obcta-an
Mr. Carlos Ocampo
Danilo M. Ocampo
Ms. Laura Bernice S. Ocampo PEC
Ms. Lorelei Ocaya
Joselito Olano
Rev. David N. Olea, UCCP
Fr. Eladio Oliver
Fr. Francisco Olvis
Rev. Temestocles Onde, UMC
Fr. Jammy Oracion
Rev. Senen Oracos, UNIDA
Jaime R. Ordioles
Edward Orilla
Sr. Evelyn Ortiz, CFIC
Flores Otik
Sr. Jane Frances Pablo, CFIC
Sr. Rebecca D. Pacete, SCMM
Rev. Joel Pachao, PEC
Pastor Raul B. Pada
Mr. Eribert Padilla
Sr. Leonidesa Padilla, FMM
Fr. Sixto R. Pahayahay, PIC
Estrellita C. Palacios
Sr. Lilia M. Palima, MSM
Ms. Rosario S. Palma
Leonilo O. Paluribot
Mr. George Panaguiton
Sr. Ma. Ludila Panaligan
Rev. Fr. Jimi B. Panares
Sr. Cres Panes, MA
Gil M. Panganiban
Fr. Michael Renes Paradela
Mr. Oliver Paraiso
Fr. Chrys Y. Parot, CEB
Fr. Bobby Parreno
Rev. David Pascua, UMC
Ma. Lourdes Pascual-Anos
Fr. Elipidio Pastera Jr.
Sr. Rufina Patosa, OSA
Sr. Mary Paul, CFIC
Fr. Eddie Pedregosa, DCK
Sr. Claire Pedro, ICM
Rev. Emil R. Perdiz
Sr. Carmelita Perez
Ms. Edna Perez
Rev. Paulo Perez
Pastor Mario Pielago
Sr. Mary Regina Pil
Ms. Marivic Pontevedra
Sr. Visitacion Preciosa, OSA
Ms. Susan Pullarca
Sr. Aurea E. Quinones, MA
Fr. Restituto A. Quintillano
Sr. Mary Esperanza Quirino, RGS
Rev. Elecito R. Qumalagan, UMC
Fr. Primo C. Racimo
Sr. Mary Radcliffe, SSC
Ms. Liwayway Rafanan
Sr. Ma. Cristina D. Ramos. OP
Dionisio Ramos
Rev. Fe Telan Ramos
Fr. Apolonio M. Ranche
Rev. Manuel Rapisura, UMC
Ms. Lucena Raquel, UMC
Rev. Fr. Marlon F. Rasgo,KAL
Fr. Lino Razon, OMI
Mr. Bern Richard Rebosura
Bernardita R. Recla
Sr. Teresita Rellosa, MM
Ms. Emelina Repuno
Fr. Joseph Requino
Tito P. Revereal, CSSR
Fr. Eleuterio J. Revollido
Rev. Benjamin T. Reyes, UMC
Fr. Bernardito Mario R. Reyes
Rev. Braille Reyes, PEC
Fr. Doroteo B. Reyes, OMI
Mariquit O. Reyes
Rev. Rex Reyes, UCCP

Ms. Gilda C. Reynes
Fr. Mario Ricablanca, OFM
Ms. Helen D. Rimando
Fr. Efren Rivasja
Sr. Helen Rivera, ICM
Ms. Teresita V. Robarios
Rev. Rudy Robles, Jr., UCCP
Gessen Rocas
Fr. Roy Roda, OMI
Anecita Y. Rojo
Fr. Jermias "Rolly" Rollon, CssR
Fr. Bernard Roosendaal, O Carm
Teresita M. Roque
Fr. Juanito Rosales, Jr.
Mr. Ronald R. Rosales
Fr. Lar Ryan SSC
Rey C. Sabio
Mr. Fructuoso T. Sabug, Jr., OIC
Sr. Jane Sadava, ICM
Fr. Benito P. Sagra, MSP
Ms. Connie Salcedo
Sr. M. Benjamin Saldava
Rev. Timothy G.C. Salem, UCCP
Fr. Pedro Salgado, OP
Sr. Lily Salilin, MSM
Mr. Isaac R. Salinas
Ms. Charlotte RA. Salinas
Nelson T. Salvador
Rev. Fr. Bernabe P. Samson, PIC
Sr. Ma. Angelina Sanchez
Rev. Avelino S. Sangon, UCCP
Sr. Lourdes San Juan, FMM
Sr. Lina Santiago
Citas Santos
Sr. Fidelis Abad Santos
Sr. Norma G. Santos, CFIC
Mr. Paul T. Santos
Sr. Celine M. Saplala, OSB
Mr. Eusebio Saranza
Fr. Ismael L. Sarmiento
Reden Sarmiento
Ma. Cecilia R.D. Sarria
Fr. Jun Sayago
Fr. John M. Scott, MM
Ms. Baby Sebial
Sr. Flora C. Secuya
Lydia Secuya
Alvaro O. Senturias, Jr.
Dr. Erlinda N. Senturias,
Rodolfo G. Sepida
Rev. Anacleto Serafica, UMC
Sr. Filomena Serrano, FMM
Ms. Fely a. Singco
Sr. Delia Marin Singian, OSB
Romeo J. Smith, Jr.
Sr. Alice Sobrevinas, OSB
Rev. Eduard Solang, PEC
Sr. Fely Solatorio
Ms. Irene Srafica, UMC
Chou Su-Ping
Sr. Mary Jeva Sumbillo, RGS
Rev. Efren Supanga, PEC
Ms. Lea E. Tabios
Cesar Tablon
Rev. David B. Tabo-oy, PEC
Evan V. Tabuzo
Teodorico Tacaban, Sr.
Ernesto F. Tadly
Sr. Eufrosino M. Tagalog
Rev. Rizalino Q. Taganas, UCCP
Prudencio Alovera Talabucon, Jr.
Zenaida G. Taleon
Sr. Christine Tan
Francis Tan
Emiliano Tanala
Mr. Dionito R. Tanion, UCCP
Fr. Ben Belmer Tano, O Carm
Ms. Jocelyn C. Tapales
Rev. Elizabeth S. Tapia
Ms. Elena Tejada
Fr. Mario John Paul Tejada, MSP
Sr. Evangeline B. Tenorio, ACT
Reynaldo A. Tero
Sr. Maryanne Terrenal

Gladys R. Tesico
Fr. Rhee M. Timbang, PIC
Rev. Jermias Tinambacan, UCCP
Ms. Jocelyn Tonquin
Sr. Rosal R. Toquilar, CFIC
Rev. Samuel Torres
Ms. Marcela M. Torzar
Mr. Jaime Jaybe Trinidad
Ms. Emelita Tuazon
Ms. Tess Tuazon
Sr. Gertrudes Tuna, FMA
Luningning Ubana
Nora Ulgasan
Juanita Umali
Rev. Marma C. Urbano
Rev. Feliciano Ursos
Sr. Mary Grace Usog, OSB
Sr. Farida Valencia, OSA
Mr. Noel Valencia
Sr. Elvira Valenzuela
Ms. Lorna O. Vugt Van
Mr. Arnold Vugt Van
Fr. Harry Eugelen Van, MSC
Sr. Consuelo Varela
Mr. Mario Vargas
Rev. Peter Vargas Jr., UCCP
Sr. Eva Varon, SCMM
Becky Vecina
Sr. Salvacion Vedar, ICM
Sr. Mila Velasco, FMM
Rev. Salvador A. Velasco
Wandrie P. Verana
Andy Veridiano
Sr. Emma Vijandre, ICM
Sr. Esther Villa, MA
Mr. Conrado Villaester
Luceno Villagonzalo
Sr. Teresita Villaluz
Fr. Ronilo Villamor
Sr. Leonila Villanueva
Marilyn M. Villanueva
Fr. Romeo P. Villanueva, OMI
Rev. Modesto Villasanta Jr., UCCP
Mr. Antonio Villasor
Sr. Emelina Villegas
Yol Vingno
Ms. Joy Vistal
Sr. Ester Vite, SCMM
Sr. Visitacion Vizon Jr., CFIC
Fr. Gil Votacion, OMI
Sr. Guadalupe Vsdez, OSB
Fr. Jack Walsh, MM
Sr. Wendelin, RM
Sr. Joan Cordis Westhues, MM
Fr. Pol Yazar, OMI
Ms. Flordeliza A. Yumol
Ms. Nenette G. Zaldivar
Sr. Aurora R. Zambrano
Ma. Nellie Zarraga
Gregorio E. Zurbano
Fr. Ton Zwart

SOUTH AFRICA

C.D. Abrahams, NG Sendingkerk
L. Abrahams, Olivet Assembly
M. Abrahams, Moravian
D.M. Ackermann, Anglican
A. Adams, Baptist
A. Adams, Baptist
J.C. Adonis, NG Sendingkerk
I.M. Ahrends, Anglican
J.J.W. Aitchison, Anglican
M.J. Alcock
A. Alexander, Congregational
N.R.S. Alexander, Anglican
E.O.A. Apelgren, Catholic
N. Aphane
D.M. Appalasamy, Anglican
L.A. Appies, NG Sendingkerk
V.B. Appollis, NG Sendingkerk
P. Arendse, Baptist
M. Armour, Catholic

A. A. Asegaai, Congregational
A.O.B. Balcomb, Anglican
D. Bailey, Anglican
B. Bam, Anglican
D. Bax, Presbyterian
J. Bester, Anglican
T. Bester, Anglican
C.P. Beukes, Chipros Community Org.
T.C. Bhengu, Catholic
A. Bhiman, Reformed Church in Africa
J.F. Bill, Evangelical Presbyterian
N. Billa, Ebenezer
R. Billa, Ebenezer
M.W. D. Birtwhistle, Anglican
M.E. Blackburn, Catholic
E. Blaser, Catholic
A.H. Blom, Belydende Kring
F. Bodibe, AEC
A.A. Boesak, NG Sendingkerk
W.A. Boesak, NG Sendingkerk
A. Boezak, NG Sendingkerk
J. Bohnen, NG Sendingkerk
T.J.B. Bonhomme, Catholic
B.G. Botha, Methodist
N. Botha, Border CC
P. Booys, NG Sendingkerk
P.J. Booys, NG Sendingkerk
H.R. Botman, NG Sendingkerk
H.J.D. Brand, NG Kerk
A. Brews, Methodist
S.B. Brittion, Anglican
R.F. Broderick, Catholic
M.A. Brown, Anglican
S. Budeli, Apostolic
K. Bugler, Catholic
R.R.V. Bulman, Anglican
E. Burroughs, Anglican
S.P. Buti, NG Kerk in Afrika
Catholic Student Association (CASA)
M.P. Cele, Methodist
C.M. Chapman, Anglican
E. Charbonneau, Catholic
F. Chikane, Apostolic Faith Mission
Christian Action Movement (CAM)
Sr. Christine, Catholic
D.R.C. Christmas, Catholic
G.D. Cloete, NG Sendingkerk
J. Cochrane, Congregational
R.C.R. Cochrane, Lutheran
A.K. Colvin, Anglican
N. Cross, Baptist
R. Crowder, Methodist
L.K. Dali, Lutheran
I. Daneel
G.F. Davies, Anglican
K.J. Davy, Congregational
M. Deeb, Catholic
G. de Fleuriot, Catholic
J.W. de Gruchy, Congregational
S.M. de Gruchy, Congregational
J. de Waal, NG Sendingkerk
J. Diale, NG Kerk in Afrika
N. Diale, N. Transvaal CC
H. Diedericks, Anglican
L. Dikene, Young Christian Students
J. Dikobo, Lutheran
T. Dingiswayo, Baptist
O. Diseko, Lutheran
J.A. Draper, Anglican
N.E. Dube, Methodist
S.W. Dube, Methodist
J.J.F. Durand, NG Sendingkerk
S. Dwane, Order of Ethiopia
J. Figland, Catholic
B.B. Finca, Reformed Presbyterian
B. Flanagan, Catholic
L. Funyufunyu, Lutheran
A. Gabuza, Catholic
S. Galane, Lutheran
R. Gallocher, Catholic
B. Gaybba, Catholic
V.T. Gcabashe, Methodist
P.C. Geerts, Anglican
B. Germond, Anglican

G.J. Gerwel, Congregational
D.J.A. Goad, Catholic
M.A.T. Goemans, Catholic
R.W.G. Goldman, Anglican
E.N. Gontsana, Church of Christ
R.G. Govender, Anglican
S. Govender, Belydende Kring
D. Govinden, Anglican
T.S. Gqubule, Congregational
D.M. Groepe, Congregational
T.Gumbo, NGK in Afrika
C.N. Gwala, Catholic
A.W. Harding, Anglican
C. Hewitt, Anglican
R. Hickley, Catholic
O. Hirmer, Catholic
M.E. Hlatswayo
J.T. Hlongwa, Anglican
M.S. Hlongwane, Presbyterian
M. Hofmeyr, NG Kerk
P Hortop, Catholic
R. Hufkie, Congregational
L. Hulley, Methodist
M. Hyam, Catholic
M.J. Inglis, Anglican
J. Irish, Anglican
C. Jacobs, Baptist
L.D. Jafta, Methodist
W.T. Jakobsen, Anglican
A. Jennings, Methodist
E. Johnson, NG Sendingkerk
C. Jones, Anglican
D.G. Jones, Anglican
J.W. Jooste, Methodist
R. Jordaan, Congregational
C. Kale
G.P. Kearney, Catholic
M. Kelly, Catholic
J. Kerchoff, Anglican
P. Kerchoff, Anglican
J. Kgabo, Lutheran
S. Khanyile, Inter-Church Youth
S.M. Khosie, Anglican
B.K. Khumalo, Lutheran
S.A. Khumalo, Presbyterian
J. Kinghorn, NG Kerk
W. Kistner, Lutheran
L. Klate, Congregational
S. Kodisang, Tswelelopele
R. Kok, Assemblies of God
I. Kolamisi, Catholic
B. Kotze, NG Kerk
J.N.J. Kritizinger, Catholic
J. Kudzingana, Lutheran
E. Kuzwayo, Anglican
E. Lafont, Catholic
E.N. Lambani, Reformed Presbyterian
C.F.J. Langefeld, Catholic
G. Landman, Lutheran
J.J. Lapoorta, Apostolic Faith Mission
B.C. Lategan, NG Kerk
C. Lazarus, Catholic
S. Lekgetho, Lutheran
C. le Roux, Catholic
A. Leruli, Lutheran
P. Lessing, Congregational
M. Linda, Old Apostolic
G. Lindegger, Catholic
I.D. Lloyd, Theology Exchange Programme
W.E.K. Loenig, Lutheran
C. Lombard, NG Sendingkerk
S.O. Loni, Reformed Presbyterian
M.P. Loveday, Anglican
L. Louw, African Methodist Episcopal
G. Lubbe, Via Christi Community
S. Luckett, Anglican
R. Lundie, Anglican
A. Maart, Congregational
J. Mabaso, Church of England
L. Mabaso, Baptist
M. Mabaso, Church of England
J. Mabuela, Apostolic Faith Mission
L. Mabusela, NG Kerk in Afrika

W. Mabuza, Methodist
E. Machaba, Lutheran
M.M. Madlabingwa, Congregational
L.P. Madlala, Catholic
D. Madiba, Lutheran
E. Mafatshe, IAG
A. Mahamba, Lutheran
C.O. Maharaj, Assemblies of God
P.S. Maharaj, Assemblies of God
S. Mahlakoane, Catholic
L. Mahlangu, NG Kerk in Afrika
R. Mahlangu, Catholic
M. Mailula, Catholic
S.S. Maimela, Lutheran
S.N. Makalima, Anglican
T.P. Makongoza, Lutheran
M.A.B. Mali, African Methodist Episcopal
E. Malindi, Church of Christ
O.T. Malindi, Church of Christ
E.G. Maliseha, Lutheran
M. Maqina, Anglican
S. Masemola, Anglican
E. M. Mashau, Lutheran
J.R. Mashige, Lutheran
S.R. Masindi, Lutheran
L. Masoko
E.M. Mataboge, NG Kerk in Afrika
T.A. Maumela, Presbyterian
M. Maja, Reformed Presbyterian
A. Majo, Presbyterian
C. Makabe, Lutheran
P. Makhubu, Baptist
E. Makue, Reformed
J. Malapane, Lutheran
A. Malema, Lutheran
D. Maluleke, NG Kerk in Afrika
J. Maluleke, Tswelelopele
E.R. Mannditsheni, Lutheran
S. Maoozoma, Anglican
H. Maphanga, NG Kerk in Afrika
M.M. Maphoto, NG Kerk in Afrika
R.E. Maraka, NG Kerk in Afrika
C. Martin, Congregational
A. Massey, Methodist
J. Maswanganyi, Evangelical Presbyterian
G.O. Matabogi, African Methodist Episcopal
E. Mateva, Presbyterian
L. Matsaung, NG Kerk in Afrika
P. Maunatlala, Student Christian Movement
L.W. Mazamisa, NG Kerk in Afrika
S. Mbande, Anglican
Z.G.M. Mbanjwa, Catholic
A. McKay, Catholic
C.R. Mayer, NG Sendingkerk
M. Mfazwa, Order of Ethiopia
K.E.M. Mgojo, Methodist
D. Mji, Methodist
I. Mkhabela
S. Mkhatshwa, Catholic
V.P.S. Mkhize, Anglican
D. Mkhondo, Catholic
T. Mkwanazi, Alliance Church
P. Moatshe, NG Kerk in Afrika
T. Modiba, Anglican
P. Modise, AEC
P. Modise, Anglican
T. Modise, Apostolic Faith Mission
T. Modise, Interdom, Youth Christian Club
K.E. Mofokeng, National Baptist
S. Mofokeng, NG Kerk in Afrika
T.A. Mofokeng, NG Kerk in Afrika
J. Mofono, Catholic
T.J. Mogaadile, African Methodist Episcopal
A. Mogase, Baptist
R.T. Mohelekete, NG Kerk in Afrika
A. Mokadi, NG Kerk in Afrika
M. Mokanyane, Catholic
M.M. Mokgatle, NG Kerk in Afrika

Z. Mokoebo, NG Kerk in Afrika
A. Mokoena, African Methodist Episcopal
F. Mokono, Anglican
T. Mokuchwane, Lutheran
S. Mokuele, Anglican
C. Molebatsi, Ebenezer
N.X. Molebatsi, Ebenezer
M.M. Molefe, Methodist
R. Molefe, NG Kerk
S.G. Molefe, Methodist
B. Moleke, Methodist
R. Moloko, African Methodist Episcopal
P. Monaisa, Interdom. Youth Christian Club
P. Monaise, Apostolic Faith Mission
R. Moningi, Lutheran
M. Montjane, Anglican
M. Morar, Catholic
M. Moremi, Lutheran
B. Mosala, Catholic
I.J. Mosala, Methodist
P. Moshiga, Methodist
T. Moshime, Catholic Student Association
M.K. Motlhale, NG Kerk in Afrika
A. Motsoaledi, Lutheran
D.A. Mpako, Catholic
P. Mphaphuli, Lutheran
C. Mphela, Methodist
M. Mpumlwana, Order of Ethiopia
R. Mpuru, Anglican
M. Msoki, Anglican
J. Mthembu, Catholic
BP. Mtimkulu, Methodist
J.L. Mualese, Lutheran
S. Mugivhi, Lutheran
A.F. Mukwevho, Lutheran
B. Mulder, Catholic
C.L. Muller, Anglican
J. Muller, NG Sendingkerk
M.T. Muneri, Lutheran
A.G. Munyai, Lutheran
T. Mutloatse, Catholic
D. Mutshiya, Lutheran
L.T. Muofhe, Reformed Presbyterian
N.M. Mvambo, Methodist
M. Mxadana, Anglican
L. Myeza
M.T.A. Naidoo, Catholic
M.N. Nair, Confessing Community Church
M. Nash, Anglican
C.F.B. Naude, NG Kerk in Afrika
B. Ncube, Catholic
B. Ndlwara, Anglican
T.S. Nedohe, Lutheran
K.C. Nemadzivhandini, Reformed Presbyterian
L.N. Nembula, Reformed Presbyterian
J. Nethengwe, Lutheran
M Ndlovu, Church of the Nazarene
R. Ngada, United Independent Believers in Christ
R. Ngcobo, YWCA
C.M. Ngcokovane, Presbyterian
E.I. Nghatsane, Presbyterian
B.N.B. Ngidi, Congregational
T. Ngoepe, Methodist
L. Ngoetjana, Full Gospel
J. Ngomane, Presbyterian
N. Ngqono, Order of Ethiopia
B. Ngubane, Reformed Presbyterian
J. Ngubane, Catholic
J.M. Ngubane, Anglican
S. Nhlapo, Apostolic Faith Mission
S. Nkanunu, Order of Ethiopia
D. Nkwe, Anglican
D. Nicolas, Reformed Presbyterian
C.A. Nissen, Reformed Presbyterian
A. Nolan, Catholic

E. Nourse, Baptist
A.E. Nsibande, Lutheran
K. Ntlha, Ebenezer
M. Ntlha, Ebenezer
R. Ntongana, Apostolic Methodist
M. Ntsele, Anglican
K.B. Nürnberger, Lutheran
R.D. Nunes, Movement of Christian Workers
D.L. Nxala, Catholic
V.Y. Nxasana, Anglican
S.M.S. Nyama, Apostolic Faith Mission
M.D. Nyawo, Presbyterian
V.G. Nyobole, Methodist
L.T. Nzimande, Methodist
J. Palos, Methodist
L.A. Parsons, Congregational
M. Pataki, Presbyterian
T. Paterson, Anglican
L.L. Pato, Anglican
R.J. Patterson, Catholic
G.S. Pegham, Anglican
R.M. Petersen, Congregational
A.M. Phaleng, NG Kerk in Afrika
N.E. Phaswana, United Apostolic
N.P Phaswana, Lutheran
R. Phillip, Anglican
M.P. Phosiwa, Lutheran
F.J.Pieterse, Inter-Church Youth
J. Pieterse, Catholic
R.M. Pietersen, NG Sendingkerk
G. Pitt, NG Sendingkerk
J. Pitt, NG Sendingkerk
A. Prior, Catholic
M. Pule, LAG
O. Pule, Apostolic Faith Mission
O. Pule, Inderdenom. Youth Christian Club
S. Pule, AEC
J. Rakgabale, Lutheran
D. Ramodibe, Catholic
G. Ramokgopa, Anglican
N. Ramokgopa, Catholic
M. Ramphomane, YWCA
N. Ramsden, Anglican
M.E. Ramulondi, Reformed Presbyterian
M.E. Ramulondi, Presbyterian
N. Rannzwa, Lutheran
S. Raphalalani, Lutheran
N.N. Richardson, Methodist
D. Russell, Anglican
W.A. Saayman, NG Sendingkerk
P. Sadie, Catholic
S. Sadie, Catholic
C. Sampson, Anglican
B. Schofield, Ecumenical Christian
L. Sebidi, Catholic
W. Segooa, NG Kerk
M. Sejake, Ebenezer
S. Sekholkwane, Ebenezer
M. Sekhopi, Lutheran
N.W. Sekiba, Lutheran
M. Seloana, NGK in Afrika
V. Seloana, Full Gospel
E. Sentsomedi, African Methodist Episcopal
P. Sentsomedi, African Methodist Episcopal
J. Seremane, Anglican
J. Seroke, YWCA
K. Seshabela, Student Union for Christian Action
W. Setati, Lutheran
V. Seloana, Full Gospel
G.M. Setiloane, Methodist
A.D.T. Shange, Catholic
F. Shayi, Jabavu Evangelical
K. Shole, Lutheran
A. Shutte, Catholic
L.N. Sibizi, Anglican
L. Siboto, Order of Ethiopia
M.E.S. Singh, Anglican
V. Sipoyo, Order of Ethiopia

A. Sisulu, Anglican
S. Sisulu, Anglican
J.Z. Skhakhane, Catholic
C. Smit, Catholic
D.J. Smit, NG Kerk
A.T. Smith, Anglican
N. Smith, NG Kerk in Afrika
T. Soeldner, Lutheran
R. Stevens, NG Sendingkerk
P.D. Strijdom, NG Sendingkerk
M. Sutcliffe, Anglican
E.M. Tema, NG Kerk in Afrika
M. Thakeli, Catholic
M.P. Thobela, Catholic
A. Tholking, Catholic
G.S. Thombeni, Lutheran
L. Thubakgale, Lutheran
B.R. Tiernan, Catholic
D.A.P. Titus, Congregational
B. Tihagale, Catholic
M. Tseke, Catholic
M. Tsele, Lutheran
E. Tshelane, United National
S. Tshitangano, Lutheran
S. Tsintsing, Congregational
D. Tutu, Anglican
J. van Eck, Congregational
W.D. van Eck, NG Sendingkerk
P. van den Heever, WPCC
C.F. van der Merwe, Reformed Church in Zambia
D.P. van der Water, Congregational
G.E. van Dyk, Congregational
P. van Niekerk, NG Kerk in Afrika
P. Vass, NG Sendingkerk
P. Verryn, Methodist
C. Villa-Vicencio, Methodist
A.J. Visagie, NG Sendingkerk
C.A. Wanamaker, Congregational
A.E. Warmback, Anglican
S. Welch, Congregational
N.J. Wentley, Lutheran
G.O. West, Anglican
A.G. Wheal, Anglican
A. Whittles, Border CC
F. Wigley, Catholic
E. Williams, Catholic
J.H.W. Williams, Catholic
J. Wing, Congregational
H.E. Winkler, Lutheran
G.H. Wittenberg, Lutheran
G.J. Wittenberg, Lutheran
B.A.A. Wood, Catholic
M.E. Wopa, Order of Ethiopia
M.E. Worsnip, Anglican
L. Xingwana, Catholic
M. Xundu, Anglican
Young Christian Students (YCS)
Young Christian Workers (YCW)
F. Zwane, Catholic

Editions of *The Road to Damascus* launched in South Africa, the Philippines, Korea and Nicaragua in July 1989.

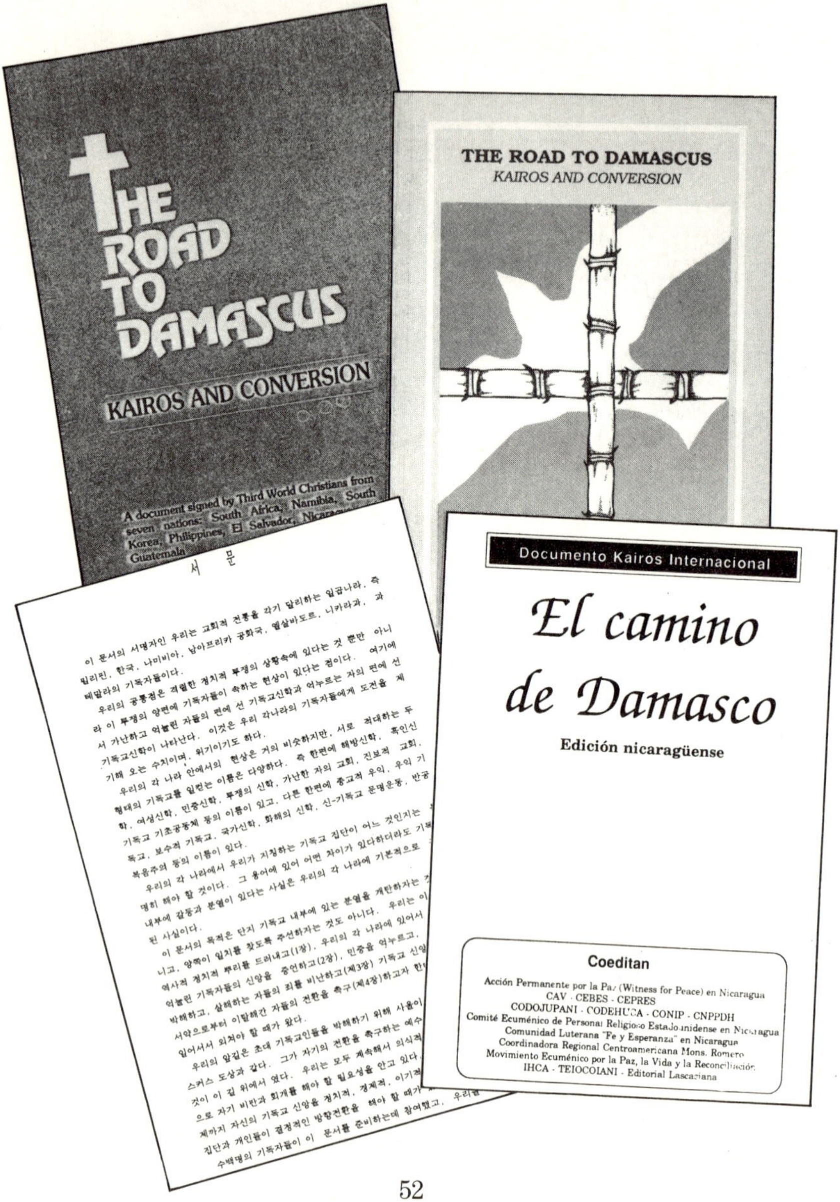